DIGITAL AND INFORMATION LITERACY ™

CLOUD-BASED COMPUTING

LARRY GERBER

rosen publishing's
rosen central®

New York

Published in 2014 by The Rosen Publishing Group, Inc.
29 East 21st Street, New York, NY 10010

Copyright © 2014 by The Rosen Publishing Group, Inc.

First Edition

Library of Congress Cataloging-in-Publication Data

Gerber, Larry, 1946-
Cloud-based computing/Larry Gerber. — 1st ed. — New York: Rosen, © 2014
        p. cm. — (Digital and information literacy)
Includes bibliographical references and index.
ISBN: 978-1-4488-9516-8
1. Electronic data processing—Juvenile literature. 2. Cloud computing.
3. Computers—History—Juvenile literature. I. Title.
QA76.585 .G47 2014
004.678'2

Manufactured in the United States of America

CPSIA Compliance Information: Batch #S13YA: For further information, contact Rosen Publishing, New York, New York, at 1-800-237-9932.

CONTENTS

INTRODUCTION

What if someone started giving away free computers, with virtually unlimited memory and all the latest software? Everybody would want one, wouldn't they?

A lot of new users would probably put their freebie right to work. They'd jump online and go about their business. Some might have a few questions. Is it for real? How does it work? Where did it come from? Is it safe? Is it really free?

Some say cloud computing is just an idea, or a collection of ideas—a business model, or a way to think about how the Internet does things that used to be done by your computer. That's true enough. But anyone who watches YouTube clips or checks movie schedules on his or her smartphone is probably using the cloud. It's real, all right.

It pays to be curious about how the cloud works because a lot of the best things there are free, and the cloud is a super-powerful computer for those who know how to use it.

Many users don't have a clue. A lot of the news about the cloud is aimed at business executives or professionals in information technology (IT), and it's written in business or technical language. The cloud is a multibillion-dollar business—actually lots of multibillion-dollar businesses. Companies are using it in all kinds of ways to offer new services, reduce their costs, and raise their profits. New companies are starting up all the time as they

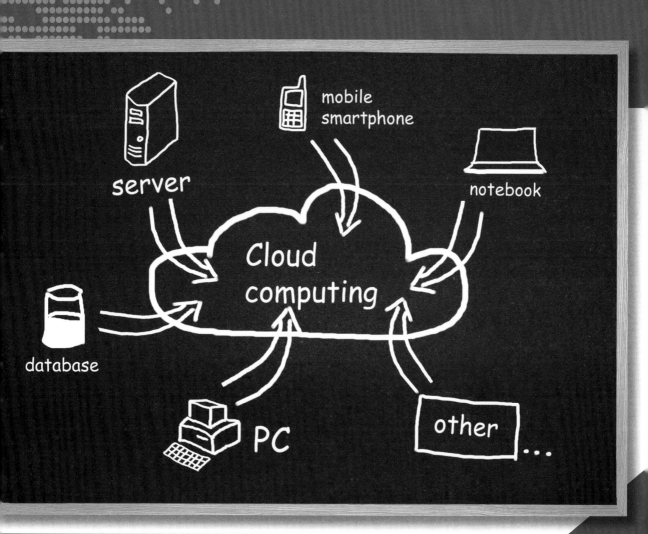

The term "cloud" in cloud-based computing probably came from sketches like this, showing how data and devices can all be linked.

develop new software and new ideas using the data and tools available in the cloud.

For most people, however, the cloud is a tool for working, playing, studying, talking to friends, shopping, building a Web site, or finding a date. It may be a place to store notes or pictures so that they're always there, even if your computer gets run over by a truck.

If the Internet can be your computer, do you even need a computer? No, but you do need a device with a Web browser, such as a phone or a tablet. That and a broadband Internet connection are the only tools you need to reach the cloud. If your files are stored there, you can use them wherever you can get online: at the desk, at the beach, on the street, at the game. That's one of the things that makes cloud-based computing different from old-fashioned desktop computing.

There are plenty of questions about the cloud. Is personal information safe there? Who else can see it? What can they do with it? Security and privacy are major issues with cloud computing, and security is a big business all by itself.

Who owns the stuff people post in the cloud? Their pictures, blogs, and stories? What are the rules? Some people think of the cloud as an example of "green" technology, but others worry that it's bad for the environment. What's the deal with that? It may take a while to resolve issues like those, but one thing about cloud computing is certain: something new is always happening.

Chapter 1

If Not for Nerds

Cloud-based computing isn't exactly the next new thing. It has been in the works for a long time, right along with the Internet. It's the result of thousands of days' work and study in labs and at keyboards all over the world. Dreamers, developers, scientists, entrepreneurs, coders, technicians, and specialists of all kinds played a part. Nerds are not known for their social life, but without them there would be no Internet, no cloud, and life today would be a lot less social.

The term "cloud computing" probably came from the cloud symbol that somebody might sketch in a diagram at a brainstorming session to show how computers, servers, databases, applications, phones, and other elements can be linked. The "cloud" can be a symbol for the Internet itself.

Punch Cards to PCs

Early computers were big, clunky machines that used punch cards for calculations. The first practical microchip was developed in the late 1950s. After that, computers were able to do much more complex calculations and do them much faster.

IBM card readers such as this one were used with early computers. The machines read information from holes punched into thousands of cards and transferred the data to computers.

Businesses and governments began to see how they could use computers to save money and improve their operations, and they began buying systems of their own. Their computers were usually kept in enclosed, air-conditioned rooms on company property, for use only by the company that owned them.

Two of the earliest Internet pioneers were John McCarthy and J. C. R. Licklider. McCarthy helped develop time-sharing systems, which allow many people in different places to use the same computing power. He suggested in 1961 that computing could be sold as a utility, much like power companies provide electricity. Utility customers don't have to maintain their own electrical generators—they take power from a grid used by everyone and pay only for what they take. This is similar to the business model used today by many cloud computer services.

Licklider believed that there would eventually be an "intergalactic computer network," and he did a lot to make it happen. In the early1960s he headed the Information Processing Techniques Office at ARPA, the Advanced Research Projects Agency of the U.S. Defense Department. He helped develop ARPANET, the forerunner of the Internet.

McCarthy's idea of computing as a service that people can use and pay for as needed and Licklider's vision of a global computer network are two of the big ideas behind cloud computing.

In 1971, Intel introduced the first microprocessors, which multiplied the power of computers. Intel engineer Ray Tomlinson wrote a program that allowed users to send messages directly from one computer terminal to another, an early version of e-mail.

Microsoft, Apple, and other computer makers were founded in the 1970s. Within a few years, there were millions of computers in use around the world, but most of them were still owned by businesses and governments. In 1981, IBM put the first "personal computer" on the market, and the following year Microsoft began licensing MS-DOS, the widely used operating system for PCs.

The World Wide Web

Tim Berners-Lee, a scientist at the European Organization for Nuclear Research (CERN), gets much of the credit for developing the World Wide Web. CERN scientists work in universities and institutions all around the world, and they needed a way to exchange large amounts of complicated data, work with it, and discuss it. Berners-Lee and others developed hypertext markup language (HTML), which is now the main language

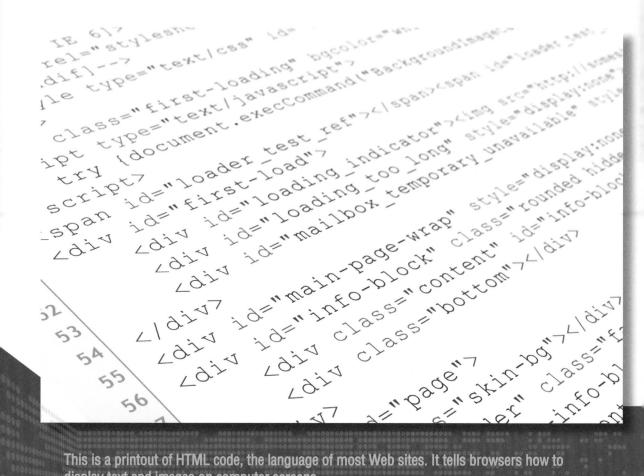

This is a printout of HTML code, the language of most Web sites. It tells browsers how to display text and images on computer screens.

of Web sites. CERN in the early 1990s released the Web for use by everyone.

It was the development of browsers that brought the Web home to millions of people. Browsers are software applications that translate HTML and other codes into the words and images on computer screens. Mosaic, invented by entrepreneur Marc Andreessen, was the first browser able to display graphics. Released in 1993, it soon evolved into Netscape Navigator, used by thousands of people as they tapped into the Web for the first time. Internet Explorer was released by Microsoft in 1995. The most

— □ X

File   Edit   View   Favorites   Tools   Help

     WHERE'S MY STUFF?

WHERE'S MY STUFF?

Storing data—tons of it—is one of the biggest uses of the cloud, and it's one of the biggest businesses.

In 2012, for example, users were uploading a reported five million photos each day to Instagram. The company, which didn't even exist three years earlier, had grown to one hundred million registered users. Facebook bought Instagram in 2012 for $1 billion.

The photo-sharing service was founded in California by a group of entrepreneurs who didn't have very much money. The startup couldn't afford to buy hundreds of computers to handle members' pictures—especially because it didn't have many members to begin with.

Instead, Instagram made a deal with Amazon Web Services (AWS) to store user data and run its apps. It was able to scale its computer services, paying only for the capacity it needed and adding more capacity as new customers came online. Netflix, Pinterest, and many other successful businesses also signed on with AWS. It's been estimated that every day, one third of all the computer users in the world visit a site that's run on AWS.

popular browsers today are Internet Explorer, Chrome, Safari, Firefox, Opera, and the various mobile phone browsers.

During the 1990s, the business world began waking up to the possibilities of cloud computing. A few small cloud-based companies became wealthy corporate giants almost overnight. IT specialists, media writers, and corporate leaders began looking at the cloud in different ways, as something that is part of the Internet but something new and different from it.

Salesforce.com set up a Web site where companies could go to find enterprise applications. Enterprise apps are tools for things like billing, managing projects, customer relations, human resources—all sorts of jobs that businesses and other organizations need to do. This was a welcome development, especially for smaller companies that couldn't afford to buy or develop their own software.

Amazon, the online bookstore, launched Amazon Web Services (AWS) in 2002, offering its unused computer capacity to other companies for data storage, applications, management tools, and other services. These commercial services aren't free. However, companies that use AWS and other cloud services can reduce the cost of running their own computers, storing their own data, and buying their own apps.

Google, the search engine giant, introduced Google Docs in 2006. Google Docs caught on not only with businesses but also with individuals.

Amazon Web Services hosts data storage, applications, and other services, making them available to businesses for a fee.

Students, teachers, engineers, designers, writers, and others can log on to Google Docs from anywhere in the world to store their data and cooperate with colleagues on their projects. Today hundreds of companies provide cloud-based services in what has become a multibillion-dollar industry.

Where Is the Cloud?

When you upload a picture to Facebook or close an e-mail, that data is stored on servers at one or more data centers, probably miles away. If you must pick a physical place to imagine the cloud, it would probably be in these data centers, also known as server farms. There are thousands of them in locations all over the world.

An engineer configures servers in a modern data center, or server farm.

Data centers have been a fixture in business offices for years. However, the server farms used by the major cloud companies are much bigger than office computer rooms. They look more like factories, and some of them really are in factory buildings, often in out-of-the-way places, with little on the outside to advertise their existence. Security is very tight, though it might not be noticeable.

Inside are hundreds of computers, mounted in rows of racks. Backup generators ensure that the center never loses power and that the industrial-strength air-conditioning never fails. The center has miles of cables as well as network gear, control software to keep data traffic flowing, and control panels to run everything.

New server farms are being built all the time to handle the explosion of data generated by the world's computer users. Some people complain that the centers spew too much pollution and waste power, and they worry that more server farms will cause serious environmental damage. Cloud companies like Facebook, Google, and Amazon are constantly looking for ways to make their server farms more energy-efficient. Cloud fans point to the greener side of things. For example, all those online shoppers who use the cloud instead of driving around spewing exhaust, or people who work at home on the cloud instead of driving to the office.

Chapter 2

Where Does Computing Happen?

People use the cloud every day without realizing it. A survey taken in August 2012 by Wakefield Research found that many Americans believed cloud-based computing involved a real cloud in the sky or had something to do with the weather. More than half the people surveyed said they never used the cloud, when in fact almost all of them were using it; they just weren't aware of it. They were banking online, shopping online, e-mailing, posting on Facebook, playing games, listening to music, watching videos . . . all examples of cloud computing.

When you read an e-mail, for example, the words on the screen are actually digital data and code stored on a server somewhere far away. What you're actually reading is your browser's translation of that data into words and images.

Browsers, Servers, and Docs

Browsers and servers are the key elements of cloud computing. Servers are usually computers that act as "hosts," providing services for people using

Many people do cloud-based computing every day without being aware of it. E-mail, Facebook, games, music, and videos are all examples of cloud computing.

other computers that are linked to them. There are file servers, gaming servers, database servers, Web servers, and other types, all named for the service they provide.

Cloud servers may fill huge data farms in remote locations, but browsers are right at the user's fingertips. They are becoming more important as the cloud grows because browsers work with cloud servers to do jobs computers used to do. It's vital to find a browser you like. Computers and phones come with browsers installed, but that doesn't mean you're stuck with the one you bought. Browsers are free downloads. It's easy to try them out and find

In 2011, Google introduced an inexpensive laptop called Chromebook, designed to work with apps and data in the cloud. Some versions were priced at around $200.

what works best. It's also important to keep browsers updated for security reasons. Some people use different browsers for their various jobs.

As more and more people use the cloud to do new things, browser companies keep updating their products with new tools. Two of the most cloud-friendly browsers of 2012 were Mozilla Firefox and Google Chrome, both with tools for Web developers. Google Chrome makes it especially easy to use the other Google cloud products, and there are lots of them.

While companies like Facebook, eBay, and Amazon have changed the way people play and shop, Google has changed the way people work

File   Edit   View   Favorites   Tools   Help

WHAT'S THAT SONG?

WHAT'S THAT SONG?

There's music in the cloud, but what is it? Shazam, a company based in London, England, was the first app maker to find a way to identify random songs from a sample of music. Shazam became one of the most popular mobile applications, with hundreds of millions of users around the world.

Hold your phone near a speaker when music is playing and Shazam takes a digital "fingerprint" of the sample. It compares the sample with millions of tunes in Shazam's cloud database. If it can identify the piece of music, it displays information such as the song title, artist, and album. Users can also get links to performances of the song on YouTube, links to buy the song, lyrics, and other information. They can share what they've found with friends on Facebook or other social sites.

Shazam gets millions of queries a week and processes so much data that it would be difficult if not impossible to run outside the cloud. The company is a big user of Amazon Web Services. Other music identification services depend on the cloud as well. SoundHound can identify songs hummed by the user.

and study. Founded in 1998 and headquartered in Mountain View, California, Google became a giant of cloud computing in only a few years. Its search engine handles billions of queries per day. The company's official mission is "to organize the world's information and make it universally accessible and useful." Its unofficial motto is "Don't Be Evil." Critics often suspect that Google might be up to no good, but the company is ranked by young professionals as one of the best places to work.

Google Docs offers free word processing, spreadsheets, and presentation programs, as well as ten gigabytes of free storage, enough to hold more than six hundred thousand pages of Word files or two hundred thousand pictures. It's possible to get even more storage by opening several accounts, although that's not encouraged unless you really need all that space.

Google Docs is making life easier for students and teachers as more of them come up with new ways to use it. It allows partners and groups to work on projects in real time. Millions of professionals around the world use Google Docs to do their work, discuss it, and save it. If you're looking for cloud freebies for schoolwork or professional work, Google is usually the best place to start. Google and other cloud companies also offer paid services for schools.

An Indiana eighth-grader who got sick and missed a day of school was able to keep up with her social studies class by logging in from home. Using a program in Google Apps, she watched the day's lesson like a slide show and kept up with what other students were doing. Some high schools and colleges live entirely in the cloud, offering courses and diplomas to anyone, anywhere. An Illinois sophomore reportedly got straight A's while sailing with her parents from Brazil to the United States. She took courses at an online high school during the five-month cruise. Web-based programs make for more interesting lessons and class projects. Students are blogging, producing videos, and building Web sites for credit.

Google's Gmail, Microsoft's Hotmail, and Yahoo! Mail are three of the most popular Web-based mail services. To stay competitive, they have to keep updating and improving their features—storage capacity, security and spam filters, searches, live chats, pictures, videos, voice, and other functions. It's a great deal for users because just about all of it is free.

Well . . . not exactly free. Google supports itself mostly through advertising. When you type in a search query or use Gmail, what you've written is scanned for keywords. The ads you see are based on the words you typed. Click on "Why this ad?" in Gmail, and the company explains that the ad "is based on emails from your mailbox."

Does Google read your mail? The company says no. The keyword searches of mail and search queries, which are used to generate the ads, are all automated and nobody at Google sees what's written. In 2010 it fired an employee for breaking its rules and reading private chats.

Sixth-graders in Sunnyvale, California, do classwork on Google Docs.

That's Entertaining!

Lovers of music and movies had reasons to smile when their favorites migrated to the cloud. The cloud's ability to handle massive data promised faster interaction and better quality in all areas of online entertainment.

Netflix started as a mail-order movie delivery service in 1997, but it took off when it introduced online streaming to members' computers and TV sets. By 2009, the company had more than ten million subscribers.

MYTHS & FACTS

MYTH The cloud isn't a safe place to store sensitive or personal data.

FACT Security is tighter at cloud data centers than just about anywhere else on the Internet. There are always hazards involved with using the public Internet to access the cloud, but major cloud operations have very high security standards.

MYTH Data centers are using too much electricity and ruining the environment.

FACT Data centers are constantly becoming more energy-efficient, and the newer ones are cleaner than older versions. Critics of air pollution near data centers don't consider the pollution that's prevented everywhere else by cloud-based computing.

MYTH Stormy weather interferes with cloud-based computing.

FACT Big storms have temporarily knocked out data centers along with other communications in the eastern United States on several occasions. But barring catastrophic natural disasters, the weather doesn't affect cloud computing.

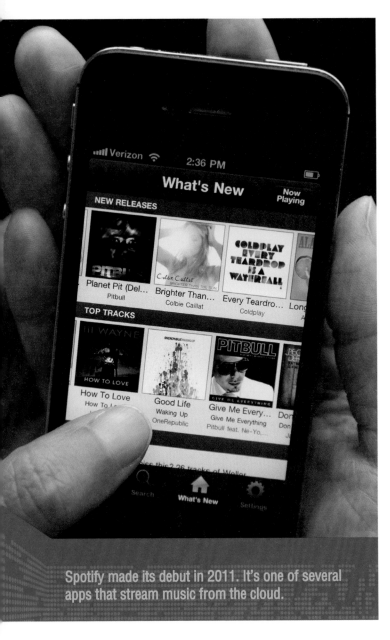

Spotify made its debut in 2011. It's one of several apps that stream music from the cloud.

Plenty of free music streams from the cloud, though it's not always exactly what listeners want to hear. Pandora is a free radio service with ads. Users can select artists and genres they like, but they have no control over what's played. Spotify radio gives listeners the tunes they choose, as often as they want, for free, with ads, on their computers. For a monthly fee, listeners get to skip the ads, and for a few dollars more, they can also get Spotify on their phones, tablets, and TV sets. Rhapsody advertises itself as the "ultimate music cloud experience." After a free trial period, users have to pay.

Even schoolwork has become more entertaining thanks to the cloud. Education companies are writing math lessons and other classwork in video game formats.

Chapter 3

Living in the Cloud

Thousands of people keep their heads in the cloud for hours at a time. Some of them virtually live there, and many will freely admit they're addicted to Facebook. In 2012, the company announced that it had one billion users, according to Forbes.com. That meant nearly half the people in the world with Internet access were using Facebook; one out of every seven people on Earth had a Facebook account. Users were uploading 300 million photos per day. The company's data centers were processing 2.5 billion content items and 2.7 billion "likes."

Whether you like the social network or find it annoying, Facebook is a household name largely because of all the ways it makes cloud computing work for its users. Like Google, it's not exactly free. Those users include advertisers who pay Facebook for access to the information you allow on its pages. The ads you see when you log in to Facebook are based on what you say about your age, hometown, relationship status, and education. Whenever you like something, that information goes into the mix as well. When you play a game or use other Facebook apps, you're telling Facebook and its advertisers even more.

Many users complain about the ways Facebook uses their information, but the social network is all about sharing. It lets other companies use its apps on their sites.

Many people don't like the idea that their information can be used by companies they don't know, but Facebook's terms make it pretty clear how things work, and it's no secret that Facebook is all about sharing. After all, its stated goal is "to make the world more open and connected." Facebook's rules for advertisers, game companies, and others who make money using it are spelled out at https://developers.facebook.com/policy. Facebook insists that they respect user privacy, and that they don't "mislead, confuse, defraud, or surprise" you.

Facebook shares much of its own information, too. You not only see ads for other companies on Facebook, you see Facebook apps on the Web sites of many other companies. That's because Facebook gives away much of the programming information it developed so that advertisers and app developers can use it on their own sites.

Mashups

In music, mashups are mixes of two or more songs, usually of completely different types of music. On the Web, mashups are sites created by programmers who mix content from two or more sites to create something completely new. They're also known as Web application hybrids. Services like Facebook, YouTube, Google Maps, LinkedIn, and Flickr publish details of the programming instructions and standards they have developed so that other developers can use them without having to write their own from scratch. These instructions are called application programming interfaces (APIs).

For example, a site called Coast Radar (http://coastradar.com) mixes APIs from Facebook and Google Maps to showcase attractions and hotels on beaches around the world. Google Maps is a favorite of Web developers because a map can be combined with just about any bit of information to make it more interesting or helpful. MapSkip (http://www.mapskip.com) is an interactive mashup created by students to tell stories about places they've visited. Users embed pictures, sound, video, or text on a base of Google Maps.

Other popular mashups combine reader opinions and reviews with lookup services. Examples are Yelp, the restaurant and entertainment finder, and Angie's List, where local businesses are listed and reviewed. Facebook, with its huge mix of apps, games, and links, is regarded by many as the Web's monster mashup.

The development of a tool known as Ajax helped bring about the boom in highly interactive sites such as Facebook and the spread of apps like Google Maps. Ajax stands for Asynchronous JavaScript and XML. It's a way of building apps so they can process user requests immediately instead of making the user wait while a whole new page reloads. Google Maps is a good way to see how Ajax works. When you move your cursor off the edge of the map, shrink it, or enlarge it, new areas of the map appear. Before the development of Ajax, the user would have to wait for the page to reload with every shift of the cursor.

The rise of highly interactive sites and the boom of mashups are part of a trend known as Web 2.0. The term means different things to different people. Sites built on user-generated content are also a big element of the Web 2.0 idea. For some, they are the only element. The business site eBizMBA (http://www.ebizmba.com) named these sites in December 2012 as the top ten most popular Web 2.0 sites: YouTube, Wikipedia, Twitter, craigslist, WordPress, Flickr, IMDB, Photobucket, Blogger, and Tumblr. They're all based on content contributed by users.

The development of Ajax led to faster and better apps such as Google Maps. "Ajax" is a combination of the terms Asynchronous JavaScript and XML.

File   Edit   View   Favorites   Tools   Help

THE PRESIDENT'S CLOUD CAMPAIGN

THE PRESIDENT'S CLOUD CAMPAIGN

Historians may look back on 2012 as the year cloud computing helped elect a president. Re-election campaigners for President Barack Obama made extensive use of AWS's cloud technology in several ways.

The campaign used an array of technology, much of it dedicated to collecting, sorting, and analyzing mountains of data on voters and voter turnout. It built more than two hundred apps that ran in the cloud.

The Democrats' cloud system included a calling tool that helped seven thousand volunteers make more than two million calls to voter prospects in the final four days of the campaign. The Republicans' system, by contract, reportedly buckled on election day because it couldn't handle the traffic.

Using data sifted from AWS, Obama for America found donors who contributed $1 billion. When the election was over, the president's team shut the whole operation down—but not before backing up their information on Amazon's storage service.

Can't We All Get Along?

A lot of the work that made the cloud possible was the result of bitter competition between business rivals. Netscape and Microsoft waged the first of several "browser wars" in the 1990s, each trying to outdo the other with newer and better versions of Netscape Navigator and Internet Explorer. The result? Better browsers and more user choice.

However, much of the innovation that led to the Internet and the cloud came from cooperation, not competition. Scientists, engineers, professors,

The Mozilla Firefox browser is an example of open-source software development.

and other experts worked with colleagues outside their countries and their organizations. Many of them didn't get paid for their work. They did it for enjoyment, for the respect of their peers, or because they felt it was important. Much of the code that makes up the language of the Internet is the result of such cooperation.

"Open source" describes products whose design and workings are available without charge for anyone to take, change, and pass on to others. The term is often applied specifically to software, meaning its source code is open to the public, and anyone is free to improve on it if they can. The Mozilla Firefox browser, the Linux operating system, and OpenOffice programs all resulted from open source development.

Web 2.0 is often described as an open source culture as well. People write blogs for free, pass around pictures, record their own songs, and build apps using the work of others in new ways without getting paid for it. They take data and apps from other sites to create mashups, which work in ways the source sites never dreamed of. The tools to do all these things are also available in the cloud for free. Wikipedia is often cited as an example of this cooperative spirit. Everything in the Web encyclopedia is written by its readers.

When some people want to compete for profit and some want to cooperate for free, there's bound to be some conflict. There's ongoing disagreement over who may own what and whether software should be free for everyone. Some critics point out that "open" doesn't mean free. They question how software creators, writers, developers, and others can go on working if they can't profit from their work.

TEN GREAT QUESTIONS

TO ASK AN INFORMATION SPECIALIST

1. What's the best browser to use with my computer for the stuff I want to do?

2. Will computers get cheaper if they don't need so much software?

3. What's the best way to back up my work so it doesn't get lost?

4. If I store my work in the cloud, who can see it?

5. What is data mining?

6. What happens to my work if data centers get wiped out by a storm or earthquake?

7. Where can I find information about cloud-based computing in plain English?

8. Where can I find definitions of the latest cloud-based computing terms?

9. Is it safe to access my cloud work from a shared computer or phone?

10. Can somebody use the cloud to track my phone?

Chapter 4

Down to Business

How did an online bookstore become one of the world's information giants? Amazon today operates big parts of the cloud, and it does many different things for millions of people and different kinds of companies.

Millions of consumers know Amazon as the company that changed the way they shop for books and then changed the way they read them. Amazon introduced its Kindle reader in 2007, and the first models sold out within hours. Readers could now download their books and carry a whole library around with them on a simple device.

In 2009, Amazon began releasing Kindle apps so people could read their downloads on their own computers. Apps for phones and tablets followed. Instead of going to a bookstore or waiting for a mail delivery, readers could now do every phase of their shopping online from start to finish. A shopper could search for a product, select it, buy it, and use it without ever looking away from the screen. Real-life bookstores soon began closing their doors for lack of business.

File   Edit   View   Favorites   Tools   Help

    HOW MUCH INFORMATION IS TOO MUCH?

HOW MUCH INFORMATION IS TOO MUCH?

Google introduced Latitude, its phone-tracking app, in 2009, and it wasn't long before users were wondering whether it worked too well. Bloggers and commenters used terms for it such as "creepy cool."

Latitude came installed on most Android phones as a check-in service, constantly updating the phone's location; users could invite their friends to share locations, and everyone could keep track of each other. The app also kept a log of where the phone had been and how long the user had spent in each place.

Potential problems were obvious. What if the user fibbed to a friend about where he or she was going but forgot to turn off the app? What if a burglar stole the phone and discovered what time the user left home every day? Could police seize phone logs to retrace a user's movements? What if the user had committed no crime but did get involved in an unauthorized political protest?

Google said it wouldn't give away user information without a wiretapping warrant, which would have to be approved by a judge. But Latitude had a hard time catching on. There were already other tracking apps with features Latitude didn't have, and Facebook already had a popular check-in feature.

Is That My Vampire?

Amazon also revolutionized the way many companies do business, and customers who sign in at http://www.amazon.com can see one of the reasons why. Every user sees a page custom-made for him or her, with recommendations for books and other products based on their shopping history. If you've been browsing for books about vampires, you'll find more books about vampires, maybe a collection of legends, a history of ancient superstitions, and a book on werewolves by the same author. You'll see what books interested others who bought your vampire book. If you start browsing for books about space flight or algebra, the recommendations will change. Vampires disappear, to be replaced by books about the solar system and math.

So what's the big deal about that? Amazon's servers simply look up your history as soon as you log in and send back their results. It happens all the time, right? Yes it does, and that's what makes it a big deal. Amazon developers had to figure out how their system could handle millions of such queries and lookups at a time without slowing down. Most customers won't

Amazon's "distributed system" of many computers led to big changes in the way people shop, and it helped make the company a cloud computing giant.

sit around for several minutes—even several seconds—waiting to see something they might want to buy, and most normal Web servers can't handle that kind of load without taking some time.

Amazon's answer was a "distributed system" of many computers, with each computer doing simple tasks in cooperation with the other computers in its network. Amazon engineers also built their system so that each computer does only the work that's needed. In a huge system like Amazon's, this meant that there was leftover capacity. Amazon Web Services was set up to sell this computer power to other companies.

Small startups like Instagram and Pinterest could make deals to pay for only the capacity they needed; as they signed up new users they could pay for more. These companies probably wouldn't have gotten very far if they had been forced to invest millions in their computer networks right from the start. Using AWS, they could scale their computer use up or down as they needed. John McCarthy, the computer genius who began the development of time-sharing in the 1960s, died in 2011. His "utility" vision of shared computer service had become a reality.

The Cloud in Business Speak

This sort of computer use and cost scaling are two of the main things that make cloud computing work for businesses. Scaling is one of several terms that are good to know if you're interested in the big picture of cloud computing. Here are several other important ones, all related to how businesses use the cloud.

- Software as a Service, usually abbreviated SaaS. These are ready-made programs that can be accessed simply by navigating to a provider's Web site. Businesses who need heavy-duty programs for their operations pay to use SaaS. However, Google Docs and the Web-based mail services are also examples of SaaS, and they're free for everyone.

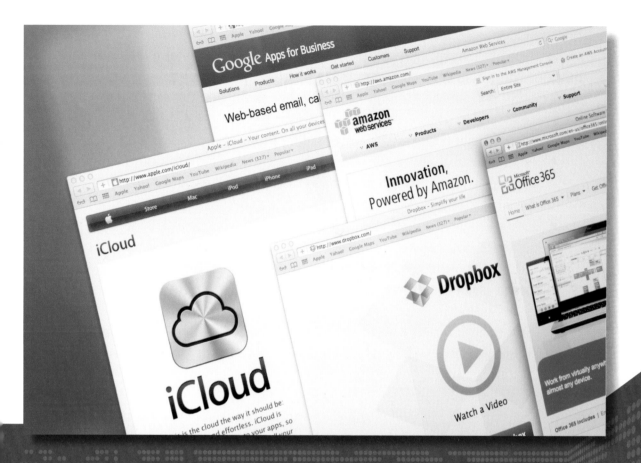

Besides data storage, these sites offer various types of cloud computing services for businesses: software, platforms, and infrastructure.

- Platform as a Service (PaaS). This is a group of services offered by a cloud provider for companies to build their own custom applications. It usually consists of an operating system, software, and servers.
- Infrastructure as a Service (IaaS). In this model, a cloud company provides storage capacity, network components, and other gear. It's sometimes called Hardware as a Service.

The computing cloud, like real clouds, can take all kinds of shapes. When experts talk about these shapes, they often use the term "deployment models"—the way organizations build their computer networks to create their own clouds and merge them with others. The main deployment models are:

- Public cloud, meaning Internet space that's open to everybody.
- Private cloud, where organizations pool their internal computing resources; these networks restrict access to the public Internet, usually for security reasons.
- Community cloud, where organizations that do similar things can set up a cloud system used by all. This saves work especially in industries where everyone has to deal with the same kinds of issues and regulations, such as health care.
- Hybrid clouds are combinations of public and private clouds; an organization might want to use a public service like Google for some of its work, while keeping its confidential data in its private cloud.

Many schools are building hybrid models because they need to work with private information as well as classwork. Personal facts about students and teachers can be kept off the Internet in servers controlled by the school district, while textbooks, lessons, and labs can be shared, even with classes in other schools and other countries.

Security Issues

Cloud-based computing has its drawbacks. Many businesses have been reluctant to adopt it for fear their data may be lost or tampered with. Besides, access to the cloud is only as good as your Internet connection; if a local Internet provider goes down, your files will still be safe, but you won't be able to reach them. Natural disasters can and do shut down cloud services for brief periods.

Larry Ellison, CEO of Oracle, talks about his company's cloud computing services. Ellison says cloud computing isn't a particularly new idea, but is something that has evolved over time.

A March 2012 study by the U.S. Federal Reserve found that just 21 percent of mobile phone users had done banking by phone in the past year. Nearly half the mobile phone users in the survey said they were too worried about security. Experts say that when a customer uses his or her phone browser to contact a bank's Web site via the Internet, hackers may have an opening to steal passwords. It's less likely, however, if the customer installs the bank's app and uses that for business, because the communication is more securely encrypted.

Other threats come from governments. Syria shut off all Internet service for its people in 2012 during a popular uprising, and other Middle Eastern governments also interrupted the Internet during the unrest known as the Arab Spring. Experts say blacking out an entire population is fairly easy to do in smaller countries, where all Internet connections usually run through a central service provider. The United States, Canada, Australia, and most European countries have many service providers, so it would be harder to cut service even if it were legal to do so.

Larger countries can interfere with service, however. China is notorious for doing so. And some European businesses have said they are hesitant about storing their data on U.S. cloud servers because American laws, originally passed to catch terrorists, might allow U.S. authorities to seize their private data.

Companies and people who want to keep the Internet open and free have rallied users to oppose government controls. These issues aren't likely to be settled any time soon, however, and fresh ones are sure to arise. As experts like to point out, cloud-based computing isn't really new. But the cloud is still under construction. Who knows what will happen next?

GLOSSARY

access The opportunity to use something; getting something and using it.

array A range or a display of things.

asynchronous Happening at different times.

byte A unit of computer data, usually an eight-number string of ones and zeroes that represents a single letter, number, or other character.

capacity The ability or power to do something; the space to contain something.

component A part or element of something.

custom Made to order for a particular customer.

data Information in digital form that's stored and processed on computers.

deploy To move resources to the places where they are supposed to work.

distributed system A network of computers that interact with each other to accomplish a single task.

donor A person who gives money to a cause or charity.

encrypt To convert data into a code that can't be read by unauthorized persons.

entrepreneur Someone who organizes a business and takes on the risks involved in order to make profits.

gigabyte One thousand megabytes.

hybrid Something created by combining two elements.

interface An area where two systems meet and interact.

megabyte About one million bytes.

scale To increase or decrease as needed.

software Programs and other data that tell a computer what to do.

spreadsheet A computer program used for accounting.

Canadian Information Processing Society
5090 Explorer Drive, Suite 801
Mississauga, ON L4W 4T9
Canada
(905) 602-1370
Web site: http://www.cips.ca
The Canadian Information Processing Society represents Canada's IT professionals. It sets industry standards and best practices, certifies
professionals, and maintains a job board.

Computer History Museum
1401 North Shoreline Boulevard
Mountain View, CA 94043
(650) 810-1010
Web site: http://www.computerhistory.org
The Computer History Museum, sponsored by Google, has programs for
students and classes, as well as exhibits on the evolution of computers,
the Internet, and the "garage lab" beginnings of today's major cloud
companies.

The Internet Society
1775 Wiehle Avenue, Suite 201
Reston, VA 20190-5108
(703) 439-2120
Web site: http://www.internetsociety.org
The Internet Society is an international organization that promotes an open
Internet that's free for all users. It sponsors leadership programs, grants,
and awards.

Mozilla
650 Castro Street, Suite 300
Mountain View, CA, 94041-2021
(650) 903-0800
Web site: http://www.mozilla.org
Mozilla is a nonprofit organization that makes Web products and
    promotes free, open source software, Internet security, and other
    causes. It encourages volunteers to help write code and work on other
    projects.

The Tech Museum of Innovation
201 South Market Street
San Jose, CA 95113
(408) 294-8324
Web site: http://www.thetech.org
The Tech Museum has galleries, interactive exhibits, and programs for both
    children and adults on technologies used in a wide variety of fields.
    Visitors can see some of the newest innovations in communication to
    come out of Silicon Valley and learn about their intersection with music,
    art, and more.

The World Organization of Webmasters
P.O. Box 1743
Folsom, CA 95630
(916) 989-2933
Web site: http://webprofessionals.org
The World Organization of Webmasters includes professionals, students,
    and teachers. It offers online training and education programs.

York University Computer Museum
355 Lumbers Bldg.
4700 Keele Street
Toronto, ON M3J 1P3
Canada
(416) 736-2100
Web site: http://www.cse.yorku.ca
The York University Computer Museum is a historical collection and a
    research center. Besides exhibits, it hosts student activities, lectures, and
    seminars.

Web Sites

Due to the changing nature of Internet links, Rosen Publishing has developed
an online list of Web sites related to the subject of this book. This site is
updated regularly. Please use this link to access the list:

http://www.rosenlinks.com/DIL/Cloud

FOR FURTHER READING

Barksdale, Karl, and Ryan Teeter. *Google Apps for Dummies*. Indianapolis, IN: Wiley Publishing, 2008.

Blum, Andrew. *Tubes: A Journey to the Center of the Internet*. New York, NY: HarperCollins, 2012.

Blumenthal, Karen. *Steve Jobs: The Man Who Thought Different*. New York, NY: Feiwel & Friends, 2012.

Briggs, Jason R. *Python for Kids: A Playful Introduction to Programming*. San Francisco, CA: No Starch Press, 2012.

Buckley, Peter. *The Rough Guide to Cloud Computing, 100 Websites That Will Change Your Life*. London, England: Rough Guides Ltd., 2010.

Crookes, David. *Cloud Computing in Easy Steps*. Leamington Spa, UK: In Easy Steps Limited, 2012.

Darbyshire, Paul, and Adam Darbyshire. *Getting StartED with Google Apps*. New York, NY: Apress, 2010.

Holzner, Steven E. *Google Docs 4 Everyone*. New York, NY: Pearson, 2009.

Miser, Brad. *Sams Teach Yourself iCloud in 10 Minutes*. Indianapolis, IN: Sams, 2012.

Negrino, Tom. *iCloud: Visual Quickstart Guide*. Berkeley, CA: Peachpit Press, 2012.

Nielsen, Lars. *The Little Book of Cloud Computing*. Wickford, RI: New Street Communications, 2011.

Rich, Jason R. *How to Do Everything iCloud*. New York, NY: McGraw-Hill, 2012.

Sande, Warren, and Carter Sande. *Hello World! Computer Programming for Kids and Other Beginners*. Greenwich, CT: Manning Publications, 2009.

Sherman, Josepha. *The History of the Internet*. New York, NY: Scholastic Library Publishing, 2003.

Windley, Phillip. *The Live Web: Putting Cloud Computing to Work for You*. Independence, KY: Course Technology, 2011.

BIBLIOGRAPHY

Amazon Web Services. "About AWS." Amazon. Retrieved November 24, 2012 (http://aws.amazon.com/what-is-aws).

Babcock, Charles. "7 Dumb Cloud Computing Myths." *InformationWeek*, November 14, 2012. Retrieved November 30, 2012 (http://www.informationweek.com/cloud-computing/infrastructure/7-dumb-cloud-computing-myths/240124922?pgno=1).

Buckley, Peter. *The Rough Guide to Cloud Computing, 100 Websites That Will Change Your Life*. London, England: Rough Guides Ltd., 2010.

Celestine, Avinash. "Cloud Computing: How Tech Giants Like Google, Facebook, Amazon Store the World's Data." *Economic Times*, May 27, 2012. Retrieved December 7, 2012 (http://articles.economictimes.indiatimes.com/2012-05-27/news/31860969_1_instagram-largest-online-retailer-users).

Cloud, Julie. *Can You Find This on YouTube?* Baldwin City, KS: Webster's Digital Services, 2011.

Cruz, Lawrence. "How Cloud Computing Is Revolutionizing Education." The Network, Cisco Technology's News Site. August 22, 2011. Retrieved December 4, 2012 (http://newsroom.cisco.com/feature-content?articleId=460910).

eBizMBA. "Top 15 Most Popular Web 2.0 Websites December 2012." eBizMBA. Retrieved December 6, 2012 (http://www.ebizmba.com/articles/web-2.0-websites).

Facebook. "Facebook Platform Policies." Retrieved November 14, 2012 (https://developers.facebook.com/policy/).

Glanz, James. "The Cloud Factories Power, Pollution and the Internet." *New York Times*, September 22, 2012. Retrieved February 27, 2013 (http://www.nytimes.com/2012/09/23/technology/data-centers-waste-vast-amounts-of-energy-belying-industry-image.html?pagewanted=all&_r=0).

Granneman, Scott. *Google Apps Deciphered: Compute in the Cloud to Streamline Your Desktop.* Upper Saddle River, NJ: Prentice Hall, 2008.

Halpert, Ben. *Auditing Cloud Computing: A Security and Privacy Guide.* Hoboken, NJ: John Wiley & Sons, 2011.

Hurwitz, Judith, Robin Bloor, Marcia Kaufman, and Fern Halper. *Cloud Computing for Dummies.* Indianapolis, IN: Wiley Publishing, 2010.

Los Angeles Times. "'Big Data' can change the world." *Los Angeles Times Opinion*, November 19, 2012. Retrieved February 27, 2013 (http://www.latimes.com/news/opinion/editorials/la-ed-data -privacy-20121119,0,7387282.story?track=lat-pick).

Matthews, Tim. "Don't Be Afraid of Mobile Banking Apps." Bank Systems Technology, September 5, 2012. Retrieved December 4, 2012 (http://www.banktech.com/channels/dont-be-afraid-of-mobile -banking-apps/2400067340).

McCollum, Carmen. "Middle School Using Cloud Computing for Down-to- earth Education." *Northwest Indiana Times*, September 18, 2012. (http://www.nwitimes.com/news/local/lake/hobart/middle-school -using-cloud-computing-for-down-to-earth-education/article_377a141f -b5f7-56e9-b3af-8dd408781e13.html). Retrieved December 7, 2012.

Miller, Michael. *Cloud Computing Web-Based Applications that Change the Way You Work and Collaborate Online.* Indianapolis, IN: Que, 2009.

Mozilla Developer Network. "Ajax." Mozilla.org, February 20, 2013. Retrieved February 27, 2013 (https://developer.mozilla.org/en/docs/AJAX).

Santos, Wendell. "Best New Mashups: October Roundup Featuring GoogleMaps, Facebook and Tumblr." Programmable Web, November 2, 2012. Retrieved December 6, 2012 (http://blog .programmableweb.com/2012/11/02/best-new-mashups-october -roundup-featuring-googlemaps-facebook-and-tumblr/).

Sosinsky, Barrie. *Cloud Computing Bible*. Indianapolis, IN: Wiley
    Publishing, 2011.
Thier, Dave. "Facebook Has a Billion Users and a Revenue Question."
    Forbes, October 4, 2012 (http://www.forbes.com/sites/davidthier
    /2012/10/04/facebook-has-a-billion-users-and-a-revenue-question/).
    Retrieved December 10, 2012.
Velte, Anthony T., Toby J. Velte, and Robert Elsenpeter. *Cloud Computing a
    Practical Approach*. New York, NY: McGraw-Hill, 2010.
Wakefield Research. *Citrix Cloud Survey Guide Partly Cloudy—About
    Cloud Computing Survey: Many People Believe "The Cloud" Requires
    a Rain Coat*. Wakefield Research, August 2012. Retrieved December
    7, 2012 (http://www.citrix.com/site/resources/dynamic
    /additional/Citrix-Cloud-Survey-Guide.pdf).

INDEX

A
Amazon, 11, 12, 14, 18, 31, 32–34

B
Berners-Lee, Tim, 9

C
CERN, 9
cloud computing
    and browsers and servers, 15–18
    and business terms, 34–35
    deployment models, 36
    and documents, 17–19
    entertainment and, 20, 22
    myths and facts about, 21
    security, 6, 21, 36–38
    server farms and, 13–14, 21
    and the 2012 presidential race, 27
computers, history of, 7–8

E
enterprise apps, 11–12

F
Facebook, 14, 15, 18, 23–25, 32

G
Google, 14, 17–18, 23, 25, 26, 36
    Docs, 12–13, 18–19
    Latitude app, 32

I
information specialist, questions to ask an, 30
Instagram, 11, 34
Internet,
    early history of, 8–9
    how cloud computing works with it, 10–13
    invention of World Wide Web, 9–10

M
mashups, 25–26
McCarthy, John, 8–9, 34
music services, 18, 22

N
Netflix, 11, 20

O
Obama, Barack, 27
open source collaboration, 27–29

P
Pandora, 22

R
Rhapsody, 22

S
Shazam, 18
social networking, 18, 23–25
Spotify, 22

About the Author

Larry Gerber is a former Associated Press bureau chief who began working with computers thirty-five years ago on the AP's private network, one of the earliest. He is also the author of *Cited! Identifying Credible Information Online*. He lives in Los Angeles, California.

Photo Credits

Cover and p. 1 (from left) Monkey Business Images/Shutterstock.com, YanLev/Shutterstock.com, leungchopan/Shutterstock.com, David Arts/Shutterstock.com; p. 5 iStockphoto/Thinkstock; p. 8 The Photo Works/Photo Researchers/Getty Images; p. 10 Soulart/Shutterstock.com; p. 12 Lionel Bonaventure/AFP/Getty Images; p. 13 Baran Özdemir/Vetta/Getty Images; p. 16 Mark Bowden/E+/Getty Images; p. 17 Bloomberg/Getty Images; p. 20 Maria J. Avila/MCT/Newscom; p. 22 © AP Images; p. 24 Till Jacket/Photononstop/Getty Images; p. 26 © iStockphoto.com/dem10; p. 28 © iStockphoto.com/piccerella; p. 33 Spencer Platt/Getty Images; p. 35 © iStockphoto.com/mkurtbas; p. 37 AFP/Getty Images; cover (background) and interior page graphics © iStockphoto.com/suprun.

Designer: Brian Garvey; Editor: Kathy Kuhtz Campbell;
Photo Researcher: Karen Huang